THE EXPERIENCE OF ANXIETY IS NO JOKE·

THE BIGGER, NA[STIER] PANIC ATTACK,

[Y]OUR HEART IS RACING,

···YOU CAN'T BREATHE,

···YOUR THROAT IS CONSTRICTED

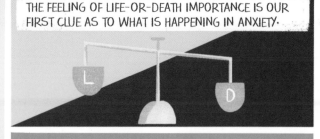

THE FEELING OF LIFE-OR-DEATH IMPORTANCE IS OUR FIRST CLUE AS TO WHAT IS HAPPENING IN ANXIETY·

THE PREMISE OF THIS BOOK IS THAT PRIMITIVE PARTS OF THE BRAIN ARE STUCK TRYING TO PROTECT YOU· YOUR BRAIN HAS BECOME TOO GOOD AT PREDICTING DANGER·

EXIT

[·]AND YOUR GUTS ARE HURTING·

IT FEELS LIKE YOU WILL DIE IF YOU DON'T ESCAPE·

EXTREME SURVIVAL RESPONSES, WITH ASSOCIATED CATASTROPHIC THOUGHTS, ARE MISTAKENLY BEING GENERATED AT THE SMALLEST STIMULI·

THE GOOD NEWS IS THAT UNDERSTANDING THE ROOTS OF ANXIETY AND LEARNING TO RELATE TO SENSATIONS IN NEW WAYS CAN HELP US OVERCOME ANXIETY·

[peop]le use "panic attack" very casually out here in LA, but I don't think most of [the]m really know what it is. Every breath is laboured. You are dying. You are going [to d]ie. It's terrifying. And then when the attack is over, the depression is still there' [com]edian Sarah Silverman 2015).

Anxiety 'is a natural reaction to perceived threat and is manifested cognitively (e.g. racing thoughts), physiologically (e.g. autonomic arousal), and behaviorally (e.g. escape).' People 'with anxiety disorders experience frequent false alarms that cause substantial distress and functional impairment' (Blakey & Abramowitz 2016).

IT'S HARD TO KNOW WHY SOME PEOPLE EXPERIENCE ANXIETY AND OTHERS DON'T, BUT HERE ARE SOME POSSIBLE CAUSES THAT HAVE BEEN IDENTIFIED BY RESEARCHERS.

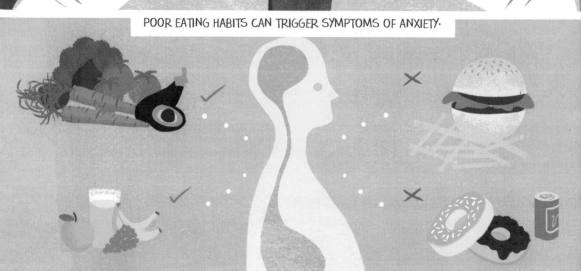

POOR EATING HABITS CAN TRIGGER SYMPTOMS OF ANXIETY.

CAFFEINE AND SUGAR ARE GO-QUICK DRUGS. THINK OF HAVING TOO MANY SHOTS OF EXPRESSO OR FEELING JITTERY AFTER A SUGAR BINGE.

COMPROMISED PHYSICAL HEALTH AND LIVING WITH PAIN ARE ASSOCIATED WITH MORE ANXIETY.

PAIN

ANXIETY

DO NOT FALL INTO THE TRAP OF THINKING ANXIETY IS JUST IN YOUR MIND.

THERE IS SOME EVIDENCE TO SUGGEST SOME PEOPLE MIGHT INHERIT A GENETIC TENDENCY TO BE MORE ANXIOUS THAN OTHERS.

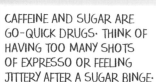

This section on causes of anxiety draws heavily on Mind's free leaflet on anxiety and panic attacks. I worked for Mind in London for 8 years. It is an excellent UK charity that offers consistently good, user-led advice and services for people with mental-health issues (www.mind.org.uk).

'Anxiety disorders appear to be caused by an interaction of biopsychosocial facto[r]s including genetic vulnerability, which interact with situations, stress, or trauma [to] produce clinically significant syndromes' (Bhatt 2017). Health always depends on t[he] interplay of biology, psychology and society (Moseley & Butler 2017).

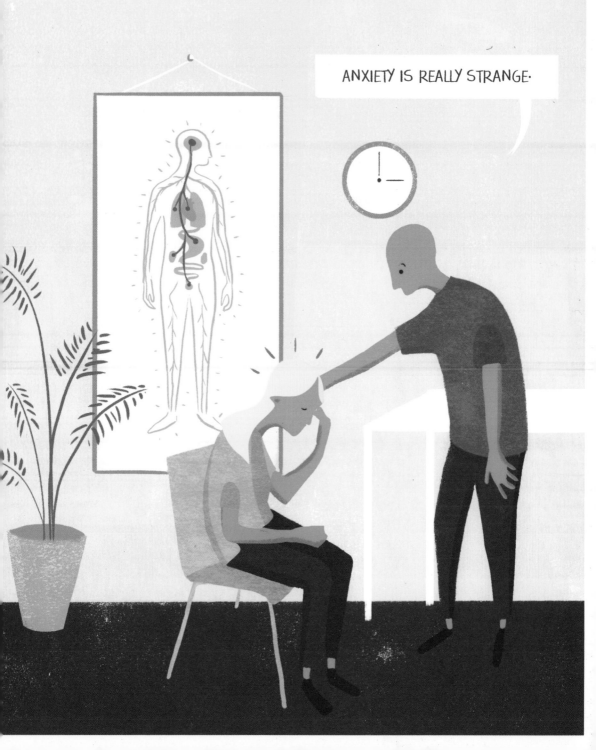

WHAT IS THE DIFFERENCE BETWEEN FEAR AND EXCITEMENT?

WHY DO SOME PEOPLE GO INTO FIGHT…

…AND SOME PEOPLE FLIGHT?

WHAT IS THE DIFFERENCE BETWEEN CAKE AND BREAD?

ANSWERING THESE QUESTIONS WILL UNRAVEL THE STRANGENESS OF ANXIETY.

ALONG THE WAY WE WILL MEET PHILOSOPHERS EXPLORING FREEDOM, MOUSE POO AND SEAT BELTS.

'Like most anxiety sufferers, my anxiety doesn't manifest itself in rational ways. So I could be with a killer and not feel alarmed but then take my dogs for a walk and be debilitated with terror they'll run into the road' (Jon Ronson (2011), author of *The Psychopath Test*, on the strangeness of anxiety).

'Anxiety disorders are the most common type of psychiatric disorders in the US. lifetime prevalence of anxiety disorders among American adults is 28.8%' (B 2017). That's more than 1 in 4 people who are seriously affected by anxiety!

ALL FORMS OF STRESS, WHATEVER THE SOURCE, ARE LINKED TO HIGHER ANXIETY.

PRESSURE AT HOME,

...WORK,

...STUDY

AND IN SOCIAL CIRCLES CAN TRIGGER ANXIETY.

£

EXHAUSTION AND WORRYING ABOUT MONEY CAN SEND US INTO SURVIVAL MODE.

ADVERSE CHILDHOOD EXPERIENCES (ACES) ARE AN IMPORTANT CAUSE OF ANXIETY. THE 'ACE STUDY' IS A LANDMARK RESEARCH STUDY, STARTED IN 1998, WHICH ASSESSES THE IMPACT OF CHILDHOOD TRAUMA.

YOU CAN CHECK YOUR ACE SCORE FROM A LIST OF 10 EVENTS, SUCH AS PERSONAL ABUSE OR NEGLECT OR LIVING IN A FAMILY WITH ALCOHOLISM, MENTAL ILLNESS OR A DISAPPEARED PARENT.

THE HIGHER YOUR SCORE, THE GREATER RISK YOU HAVE OF POOR MENTAL AND PHYSICAL HEALTH.

'here are 10 types of childhood trauma measured in the ACE Study... Each type of 'auma counts as one. So a person who's been physically abused, with one alcoholic 'arent, and a mother who was beaten up has an ACE score of three' (from the 'onderful www.acestoohigh.com).

'1 in 8 people have 4 or more ACEs... For a person with an ACE score of four or more, their relative risk of chronic obstructive pulmonary disease was two and a half times that of someone with an ACE score of zero. ... For depression, it was four and a half times' (Dr Burke Harris 2015).

MOUSE POO ALERT! HERE IS A MIND-BOGGLING EXPERIMENT THAT SHOWS US HOW MUCH WE HAVE TO LEARN ABOUT MIND-BODY INTERACTION.

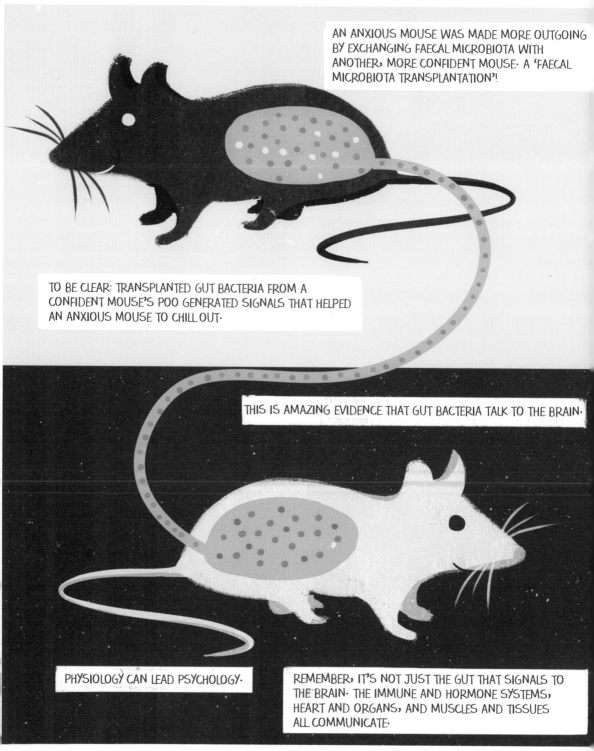

AN ANXIOUS MOUSE WAS MADE MORE OUTGOING BY EXCHANGING FAECAL MICROBIOTA WITH ANOTHER, MORE CONFIDENT MOUSE: A 'FAECAL MICROBIOTA TRANSPLANTATION'!

TO BE CLEAR: TRANSPLANTED GUT BACTERIA FROM A CONFIDENT MOUSE'S POO GENERATED SIGNALS THAT HELPED AN ANXIOUS MOUSE TO CHILL OUT.

THIS IS AMAZING EVIDENCE THAT GUT BACTERIA TALK TO THE BRAIN.

PHYSIOLOGY CAN LEAD PSYCHOLOGY.

REMEMBER, IT'S NOT JUST THE GUT THAT SIGNALS TO THE BRAIN. THE IMMUNE AND HORMONE SYSTEMS, HEART AND ORGANS, AND MUSCLES AND TISSUES ALL COMMUNICATE.

There is growing evidence in humans and in mice that 'the intestinal microbiome influences the brain and behavior', i.e. there is a 'gut microbiome-to-brain axis' (Collins et al 2013). 'Gut-brain communication' links 'anxiety disorders and... inflammatory bowel disease' (Neufeld et al 2011; Temperton 2015).

'Some of the most devastating medical and public health problems of our time depression, substance addiction and intractable pain - are centred on pathologies feeling' (Damasio et al 2013). Good news: Craig (2015) states 'Your interocepti awareness is key to everything. It can be trained.'

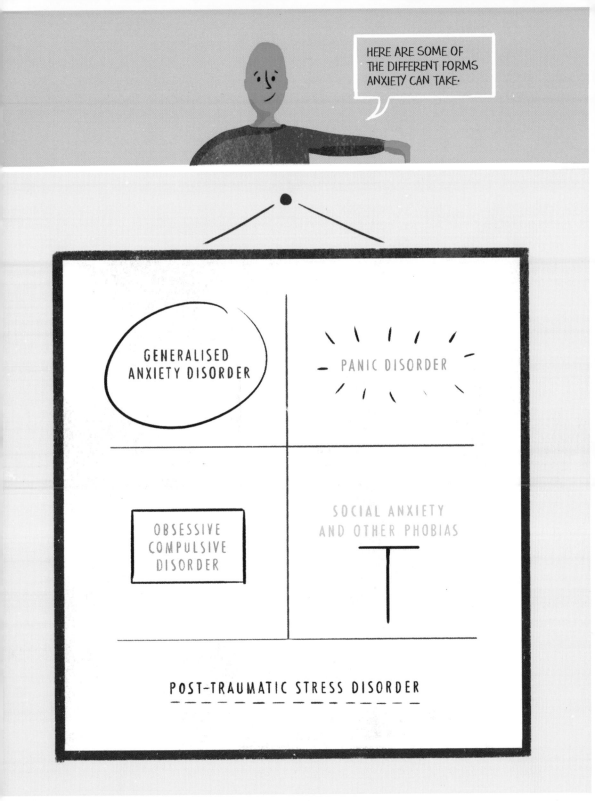

Generalised anxiety disorder (GAD) includes a wide range of symptoms, but involves non-specific anxiety for extended periods. Your 'experience with GAD might be quite different from the problems another person experiences'. 'Panic disorder can mean that you feel constantly afraid of having another panic attack' (Mind 2017).

In OCD, 'unwelcome thoughts' that 'repeatedly appear in your mind' exist with 'repetitive activities that you feel you have to do'. 'If you have a phobia, your anxiety may be triggered by very specific situations or objects.' PTSD 'can feel like you're reliving all the fear and anxiety you experienced' during a trauma (Mind 2017).

LET'S EXPLORE SOME REALLY BIG IDEAS AND CHALLENGES.

THE PHILOSOPHER KIERKEGAARD OFFERED THAT 'ANXIETY IS THE DIZZINESS OF FREEDOM'.

HOPES

FEARS

PREDICTIONS

WE ARE NOT UNTHINKING, BRUTE ANIMALS THAT JUST REACT. WE HAVE MEMORIES, HOPES, FEARS AND THE ABILITY TO PREDICT FUTURE EVENTS.

THE GIFT OF SELF-AWARENESS PERMITS A SPACE BETWEEN ACTION AND REACTION. THERE IS A GAP THAT WE CAN OCCUPY WHERE WE FEEL WE HAVE CHOICE.

ACTION

REACTION

THAT GAP IS OFTEN FLEETING AND FULL OF FEAR. THE CONTEMPLATIVE SPACE AFTER CHOOSING IS FREQUENTLY FULL OF DOUBT: 'HAVE I DONE THE RIGHT THING?' 'HOW WILL I BE JUDGED?'

Bakewell (2017), discussing Kierkegaard: 'constant choosing brings a pervasive anxiety, not unlike the vertigo that comes from looking over a cliff. It is not the fear of falling so much as the fear that you can't trust yourself not to throw yourself off.'

'*The Second Sex* was almost entirely occupied with the complex territory where free choice, biology and social and cultural factors meet and mingle to create a human being who gradually becomes set in her ways as life goes on' (Bakewell 2017 on Simone de Beauvoir).

FREEDOM DEEPLY OCCUPIED EXISTENTIALISTS SUCH AS JEAN-PAUL SARTRE AND SIMONE DE BEAUVOIR. WRITING IN THE SECOND WAR, IN A PARIS OCCUPIED BY THE NAZIS, THEY FORMULATED SOME SURPRISING IDEAS.

THERE IS AN 'EXISTENTIAL ANXIETY THAT COMES WITH CONSIDERING OURSELVES FREE AGENTS WHO ARE RESPONSIBLE FOR WHAT WE DO.'

THERE ARE LIMITS FROM HABITS, BIOLOGY, SOCIETY AND CULTURE.

HOWEVER, WE ARE ESSENTIALLY FREE TO CHOOSE HOW WE MEET OUR SITUATION.

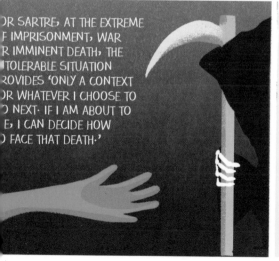

OR SARTRE, AT THE EXTREME F IMPRISONMENT, WAR R IMMINENT DEATH, THE TOLERABLE SITUATION ROVIDES 'ONLY A CONTEXT OR WHATEVER I CHOOSE TO O NEXT. IF I AM ABOUT TO E, I CAN DECIDE HOW O FACE THAT DEATH.'

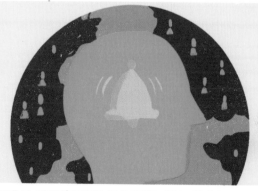

THIS IS HEADY STUFF. IT SHOWS ANXIETY IS A BIG, CONFUSING PROBLEM CENTRAL TO BEING HUMAN. YOU ARE CERTAINLY NOT ALONE IN FEELING ANXIOUS.

es, influences and habits can accumulate over a lifetime to create a structure becomes hard to break out of' (this, and other quotes above, from Bakewell). We are free to the extent that oppressive power structures, economics and al norms allow.

'History, despite its wrenching pain, cannot be unlived, but if faced with courage, need not be lived again.' The incomparable Maya Angelou (1993) reminds us that courage is needed to transcend our past.

SIMONE DE BEAUVOIR IS FAMOUS FOR QUESTIONING THE BIOLOGICAL CERTAINTY OF GENDER: 'ONE IS NOT BORN, BUT RATHER BECOMES, A WOMAN.'

ANXIETY

IF SOMETHING AS SEEMINGLY FIXED AS GENDER CAN BE SHAPED AND FORMED, THEN WE CAN BE HOPEFUL THAT THE RESPONSE TO THE PHYSIOLOGY UNDERPINNING ANXIETY CAN ALSO BE SHAPED AND REFORMED.

EXISTENTIAL PHILOSOPHY OFFERS HOPE AND A CHALLENGE.

THE CHALLENGE: TAKING RESPONSIBILITY FOR THE DIFFICULT PROCESS OF DECONSTRUCTING THE STRUCTURES THAT BIND US.

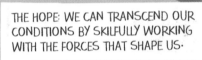

THE HOPE: WE CAN TRANSCEND OUR CONDITIONS BY SKILFULLY WORKING WITH THE FORCES THAT SHAPE US.

WE WILL LEARN THAT CURRENT NEUROSCIENCE, SPECIFICALLY THE MODEL OF CONSTRUCTED EMOTION, HELPS US EMBRACE A 'RADICAL FREEDOM' TO BE MORE THAN OUR BIOLOGY. WE CAN BE MORE THAN OUR ANXIETY.

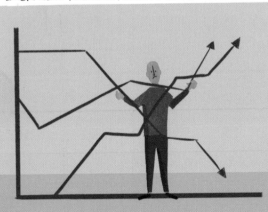

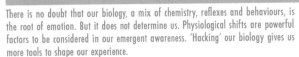

There is no doubt that our biology, a mix of chemistry, reflexes and behaviours, is the root of emotion. But it does not determine us. Physiological shifts are powerful factors to be considered in our emergent awareness. 'Hacking' our biology gives us more tools to shape our experience.

'Radical freedom' is a liberating Sartre phrase that is deeply hopeful when applied individuals. The existentialists were also intensely concerned with politics and 'su mechanisms of oppression'; freedom is 'the topic underlying all others' and is personal and political (Bakewell 2017).

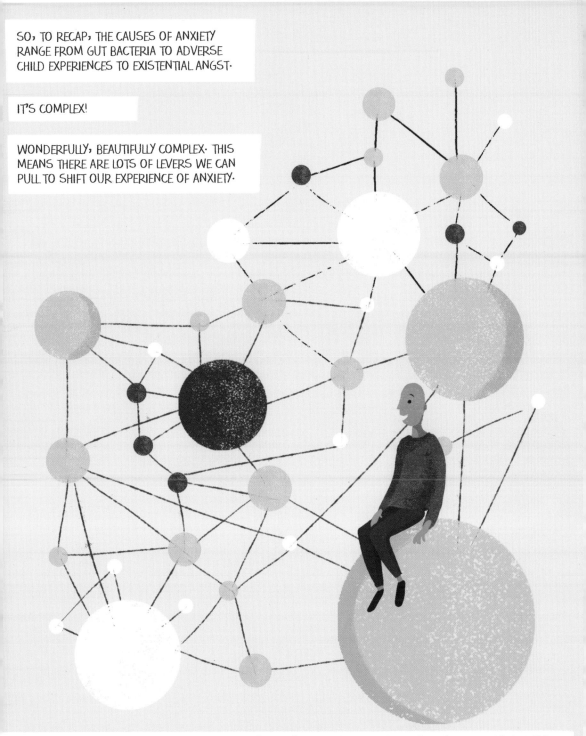

SO, TO RECAP, THE CAUSES OF ANXIETY RANGE FROM GUT BACTERIA TO ADVERSE CHILD EXPERIENCES TO EXISTENTIAL ANGST.

IT'S COMPLEX!

WONDERFULLY, BEAUTIFULLY COMPLEX. THIS MEANS THERE ARE LOTS OF LEVERS WE CAN PULL TO SHIFT OUR EXPERIENCE OF ANXIETY.

THE CORE MODEL OFFERED HERE IS THAT ANXIETY ALWAYS INVOLVES GETTING STUCK IN PROTECTIVE DEFENSE CASCADES OF 'FIGHT-OR-FLIGHT' OR 'FREEZE'. THE PERCEPTION OF THREAT CAN BE TRIGGERED BY EVENTS INSIDE THE BODY, INSIDE THE MIND OR FROM THE ENVIRONMENT.

bert Saplosky (2017): 'you're not going to get anywhere if you think there's going be the brain region or the hormone or the gene or the childhood experience or the olutionary mechanism that explains everything. Instead, every bit of behavior has ultiple levels of causality.'

'The brain areas and neuromodulatory systems that contribute to fear and anxiety exhibit great overlap' (Tovote et al 2015). Kozlowska et al (2015) describe 'the defence cascade'; anxiety is associated with mobilisation (fight-or-flight) and immobilisation (freeze/dissociation); prior learning affects whether you fight or flee or freeze.

WHAT IS AN EMOTION?

THE STUDY OF EMOTION CAN HELP US TO UNDERSTAND ANXIETY AND LAYS THE GROUNDWORK FOR HOW WE CAN CHANGE ANXIETY.

THE VICTORIANS, WITH THEIR STIFF UPPER LIPS, PRIVILEGED RATIONALITY OVER EMOTION. TO BE EMOTIONAL WAS CLOSE TO BEING HYSTERICAL. OVERT EXPRESSIONS OF EMOTION WERE SIGNS OF WEAKNESS.

THE MYTH THAT EMOTION AND REASON ARE SEPARATE PERSISTS TO THIS DAY. THINK MR SPOCK FROM *STAR TREK*.

CHARLES DARWIN AND THE PHILOSOPHER WILLIAM JAMES WERE AMONG THE FIRST RIGOROUS INVESTIGATORS OF EMOTION.

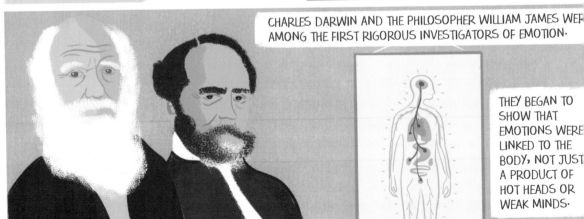

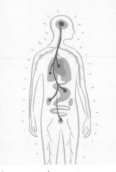

THEY BEGAN TO SHOW THAT EMOTIONS WERE LINKED TO THE BODY, NOT JUST A PRODUCT OF HOT HEADS OR WEAK MINDS.

'A human being in perfection ought always to preserve a calm and peaceful mind, and never allow passion or a transitory desire to disturb his tranquillity' (Mary Shelley 1818). Her classic Victorian gothic novel *Frankenstein* can be seen as a complex exploration of the consequences of unbalanced rationality and excess emotion.

'Darwin argued that...emotional expressions are not just universal across cultures, but their roots in purposeful, and similar, animal behaviours across many mammilian sp Darwin's basic thesis helped 'usher forth the robust scientific study of emotional expe and 'has been elaborated, refined, studied and debated ever since' (Zolli 2015)

'FEELING' IS A BEAUTIFUL WORD IN ENGLISH. IT IS USED TO DESCRIBE PHYSICAL SENSATIONS, AS IF SOMETHING IS BEING TOUCHED: 'I FEEL WARM.'

IT IS ALSO USED FOR AN EMOTIONAL STATE OR REACTION: 'I FEEL HAPPY.'

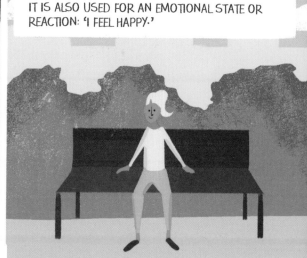

IN ORDINARY LANGUAGE THERE IS FREQUENTLY NO DIFFERENCE BETWEEN AN EMOTION AND A FEELING.

THE METAPHORS WE USE FOR EMOTIONS SHOW US THAT THE SEPARATION OF MIND AND BODY IS A MYTH. WHO HAS NOT HAD THEIR 'HEART BROKEN', EVEN JUST A LITTLE BIT?

OR STRUGGLED TO MAKE A 'GUT-WRENCHING' DECISION?

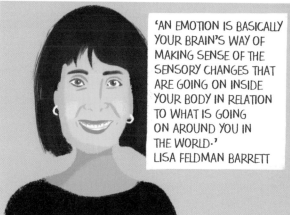

'AN EMOTION IS BASICALLY YOUR BRAIN'S WAY OF MAKING SENSE OF THE SENSORY CHANGES THAT ARE GOING ON INSIDE YOUR BODY IN RELATION TO WHAT IS GOING ON AROUND YOU IN THE WORLD.'
LISA FELDMAN BARRETT

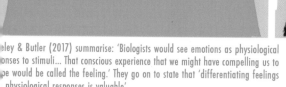

...eley & Butler (2017) summarise: 'Biologists would see emotions as physiological ...onses to stimuli... That conscious experience that we might have compelling us to ...pe would be called the feeling.' They go on to state that 'differentiating feelings ...physiological responses is valuable'.

Scientists use a confusing mix and match of terms. For body phenomena: 'physiology', 'behaviour', 'reflexes', 'affect' (Barrett 2017), 'drives', 'emotions' (Damasio et al 2013). For awareness of body phenomena: 'emotions' (Barrett 2017), 'feelings' (Damasio et al 2013), 'homeostatic emotions' (Craig 2015).

BRAINS ARE FUNDAMENTALLY CONCERNED WITH TWO THINGS. 'AM I SAFE?'

AND 'HOW CAN I CONSERVE CALORIES?'

ALL EMOTIONS ARE BASED ON EVALUATIONS OF THE AROUSAL STATE OF THE BODY (QUICK OR CALM) AND THE VALENCE (MESSAGES OF ADVANTAGE/LIKE OR DANGER/DISLIKE).

WE HAVE HUGE AMOUNTS OF INFORMATION FLOWING FROM OUR BODY THROUGH OUR BRAIN.

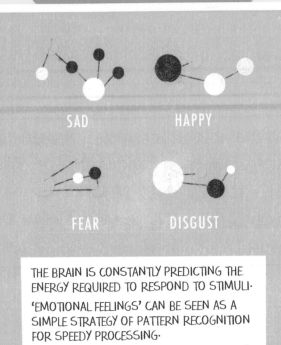

SAD

HAPPY

FEAR

DISGUST

THE BRAIN IS CONSTANTLY PREDICTING THE ENERGY REQUIRED TO RESPOND TO STIMULI.

'EMOTIONAL FEELINGS' CAN BE SEEN AS A SIMPLE STRATEGY OF PATTERN RECOGNITION FOR SPEEDY PROCESSING.

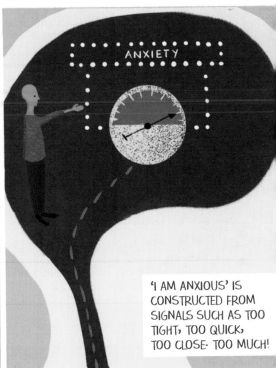

ANXIETY

'I AM ANXIOUS' IS CONSTRUCTED FROM SIGNALS SUCH AS TOO TIGHT, TOO QUICK, TOO CLOSE. TOO MUCH!

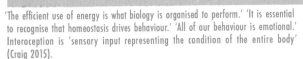

'The efficient use of energy is what biology is organised to perform.' 'It is essential to recognise that homeostasis drives behaviour.' 'All of our behaviour is emotional.' Interoception is 'sensory input representing the condition of the entire body' (Craig 2015).

'A feeling is an interoceptive construct that the brain uses to represent the ove energy costs and benefits of any actual or potential emotional behavior, the homeostatic valuation' (Craig 2015). 'Emotional states are automatic signal danger and advantage' (Damasio and Le Doux 2013).

ARE EMOTIONS HARD-WIRED INTO THE BODY AND BRAIN, TRANSCENDING CULTURE AND SPECIES? OR, ARE EMOTIONS LEARNED AND CONTEXT DEPENDENT? THIS ONGOING DEBATE IS A VERSION OF 'NATURE' VERSUS 'NURTURE'.

NATURE

NURTURE

HIGHLY INFLUENTIAL WORK BY PAUL ECKMAN OFFERED THAT EMOTIONS ARE ESSENTIALLY THE SAME FOR ALL HUMAN BEINGS.

IN THE 'NATURE' MODEL, OUR FACES, BODIES AND BRAINS ACT OUT PATTERNS HONED BY EVOLUTION.

THERE IS A HIERARCHY OF BODY-EMOTION-COGNITION.

HARD-WIRED CIRCUITS INSIDE THE BRAIN ARE SAID TO COMPETE TO GENERATE DISTINCT EMOTIONS SUCH AS FEAR, DISGUST, ANGER, JOY, SADNESS.

THE CHALLENGE TO THE HARD-WIRED MODEL IS THE SHEER VARIETY OF WAYS THAT WE CAN EXPRESS EMOTIONS.

WE CAN CLENCH OUR FISTS IN HAPPINESS AS OUR TEAM WINS. WE CAN DISSOLVE IN HAPPINESS AT THE CARESS OF A LOVER. WE CAN EVEN CRY WITH HAPPINESS.

A QUICK DETOUR TO SHOW ANXIETY IS NOT ALL BAD.

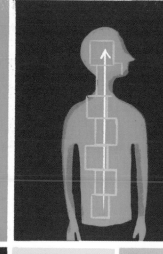

...an showed pictures of actors' faces to hunter-gatherers in Papua New Guinea. He ...med they were able to name the distinct, universal emotions shaped by evolution. 'Facial Action Coding System' analyses face muscles to create 'the first objective ...sure of specific emotion' (Keltner 2009).

The variability in expression 'suggests that emotions are as much cultural signals as they are biological ones' (Zolli 2015). Barrett (2017) critiques Ekman; attempts to replicate his research in Namibia did not work, she is damning on using actors' faces and the priming of subjects in the original studies.

'ANXIETY IS A GOOD THING BECAUSE PSYCHOPATHS DON'T HAVE ANY.' JON RONSON

ANXIETY IS A NORMAL FEATURE OF BEING HUMAN, WITHOUT IT WE CAN BECOME COLD AND CALCULATING. JON RONSON'S AMAZING QUOTE SUGGESTS THAT A LACK OF ANXIETY IS A TRAIT OF PSYCHOPATHY!

ANXIETY CAN BE GOOD· IT HELPS US PREPARE AND NOT BE OVERCONFIDENT·

INFLUENTIAL RESEARCH FROM 1908 SHOWED THAT A LITTLE BIT OF ANXIETY AND AROUSAL HELPS US PERFORM BETTER· TRY REFRAMING 'I AM ANXIOUS' TO 'THERE IS A PROTECTIVE FEELING OF GETTING READY FOR ACTION'· NOT QUITE AS SNAPPY, BUT MUCH MORE USEFUL·

LISA FELDMAN BARRETT PROPOSES A NON-HIERARCHICAL 'NURTURE' MODEL THAT CELEBRATES COMPLEXITY. EMOTIONS ARE CONSTRUCTED USING CONCEPTS.

CONCEPTS HELP US DECIDE WHETHER SOMETHING IS CAKE OR BREAD.

CAKE IS MADE FROM CLASSIC INGREDIENTS OF SUGAR, FLOUR, EGGS AND BUTTER.

THERE IS A HUGE VARIETY OF CAKES, FROM BLACK FOREST GATEAU TO CARROT CAKE.

WE CAN MAKE A POLENTA CAKE WITH CORN, MAPLE SYRUP AND COCONUT OIL – NONE OF THE CLASSIC INGREDIENTS BUT STILL, WE AGREE, IT FITS THE CONCEPT OF CAKE.

BRIOCHE IS ALSO MADE FROM SUGAR, FLOUR, EGGS AND BUTTER. DELICIOUS. BUT, WE AGREE, IT'S A TYPE OF BREAD.

A QUICK HEART, BRACED MUSCLES, AN ADRENALINE SURGE, CHURNING GUTS ARE ALL-PURPOSE INGREDIENTS USED IN MANY EMOTIONS.

FEAR   EXCITEMENT

FEAR AND EXCITEMENT USE SIMILAR INGREDIENTS, JUST LIKE BREAD AND CAKE, BUT THE EXPERIENCE IS VERY DIFFERENT ACCORDING TO THE CONCEPT WE APPLY.

For simple tasks, increasing arousal continues to help us to be more focused, but, after helping initially, unchecked arousal 'impairs performance under more complex or challenging learning situations' (Diamond et al 2007 commenting on the influential Yerkes-Dobson graph from 1908).

'Emotions are not built-in but made from more basic parts. They are not universal vary from culture to culture. They are not triggered; you create them. They emerge combination of the physical properties of your body, a flexible brain that wires itse whatever environment (culture and upbringing) it develops in' (Barrett 2017).

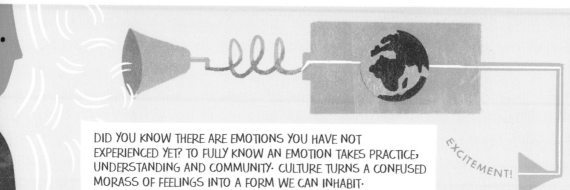

DID YOU KNOW THERE ARE EMOTIONS YOU HAVE NOT EXPERIENCED YET? TO FULLY KNOW AN EMOTION TAKES PRACTICE, UNDERSTANDING AND COMMUNITY. CULTURE TURNS A CONFUSED MORASS OF FEELINGS INTO A FORM WE CAN INHABIT.

EXCITEMENT!

GERMAN
SCHADENFREUDE

IN ENGLISH THERE IS NO EQUIVALENT WORD TO THE GERMAN 'SCHADENFREUDE'. THE PACKAGE 'JOY AT ANOTHER'S DISCOMFORT' IS NOVEL FOR ENGLISH SPEAKERS.

DANISH
HYGGE

'HYGGE' IS A DANISH WORD THAT SUMMARISES A STATE OF COSINESS, EASE AND COMFORT THAT DANES INSTANTLY GET, BUT NON-DANES HAVE TO WORK OUT.

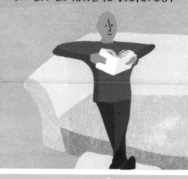

HEBREW
FIRGUN

'FIRGUN' IS 'DELIGHT IN ANOTHER'S SUCCESS' IN HEBREW.

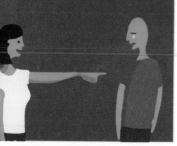

FILIPINO
LIGET

'LIGET' IS AN EMOTION THAT ANTHROPOLOGIST RENATO ROSALDO STRUGGLED TO GRASP WHILE LIVING WITH AN ISOLATED FILIPINO TRIBE IN THE 1960S. IT WAS USED FOR ENERGETIC 'BOUNDING UP A TRAIL', 'COLLECTIVE GRIEF' AND 'UNMOORED' CHAOTIC VIOLENCE.

YEARS LATER, THE MEANING SHIFTED FOR ROSALDO, FROM A 'STERILE' UNDERSTANDING TO A LIVED EXPERIENCE. IN THE INTENSITY OF HOWLING OVER THE DEATH OF HIS WIFE, HE DISCOVERED LIGET AS 'HIGH-VOLTAGE' ALIVENESS.

brain makes emotion as it needs it, on the spot, using a set of all-purpose edients. So the same brain networks that make emotion also make thoughts, and nories and perceptions' (Barrett 2017). 'Liget' quotes are from an interview with ato Rosaldo, Invisibilia on NPR (Spiegel 2017).

'Perception...has to be a process of informed guesswork in which the brain combines sensory signals with its prior expectations or beliefs about the way the world is to form its best guess of what caused those signals.' 'We don't just passively perceive the world, we actively generate it' (Seth 2017).

THE CONSTRUCTED EMOTION MODEL STATES THAT EMOTIONS ARE NOT HARD-WIRED.

THEY ARE NOT PART OF AN UNSTABLE HIERARCHY SANDWICHED BETWEEN BODY AND COGNITION.

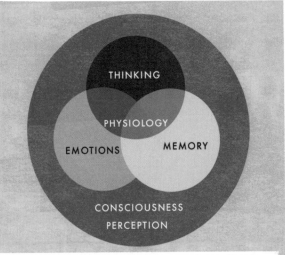

THINKING

PHYSIOLOGY

EMOTIONS

MEMORY

CONSCIOUSNESS

PERCEPTION

EMOTIONS ALWAYS CO-EMERGE WITH MEMORY AND THINKING. FEELINGS ARE ALWAYS PART OF PERCEPTION AND ARE FUNDAMENTAL TO CONSCIOUSNESS.

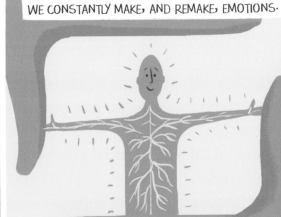

WE CONSTANTLY MAKE, AND REMAKE, EMOTIONS.

WE DO NOT HAVE TO BECOME VICTIMS OF FLAWED 'EMOTION CIRCUITS'. THERE AREN'T ANY. WE CAN REFRAME OUR EXPERIENCE.

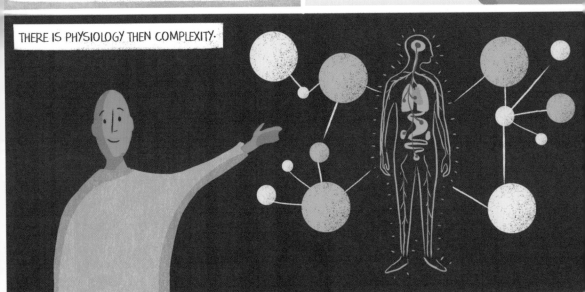

THERE IS PHYSIOLOGY THEN COMPLEXITY.

BRAINS PREDICT AND PROTECT.
WE ARE QUICK TO PREDICT DISASTER, USING OUR WORST MEMORIES AS A TEMPLATE.

IN ANXIETY WE ARE ALWAYS READY WITH THE FINGER ON THE BIG RED BUTTON. THE BUTTON THAT SHOULD BE PRESERVED FOR LIFE-OR-DEATH SITUATIONS.

THIS IS THE PROBLEM OF ANXIETY DISORDERS (AND PERSISTENT PAIN, TIREDNESS, CHRONIC INFLAMMATION AND DISSOCIATION).

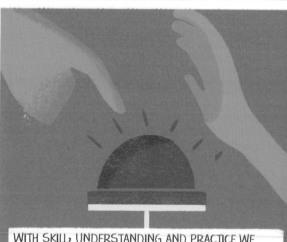

WITH SKILL, UNDERSTANDING AND PRACTICE WE CAN CATCH THE ALARM SYSTEMS IN ACTION. WE CAN NEGOTIATE, ORIENT TO WHAT IS ACTUALLY HAPPENING AND ACT OUT A NEW POSSIBILITY.

REMEMBER, HOWEVER, THE DANGER SENSORS GO DEEP. WE NEED TO MANAGE THE COMPLEX INTERPLAY OF PHYSIOLOGICAL REFLEXES, FAMILY TRIGGERS AND OPPRESSIVE CULTURE.

POSSIBLE, BUT HARD.
THE REST OF THE BOOK EXPLORES SOME RESEARCH-BASED TOOLS THAT CAN HELP.

GROUNDING IS THE FIRST TOOL: PUT DOWN SOME ROOTS AND WAKE YOUR BODY UP.

GROUNDING IS ABOUT FINDING SAFETY AND CONNECTION IN THE PRESENT MOMENT. AND, ESSENTIALLY, GROUNDING IS ABOUT CONNECTION TO THE BODY.

IT CAN TAKE TIME. SO, AT THE START, ANYTHING THAT HELPS ESTABLISH SAFETY IS USEFUL: THAT MAY INCLUDE BEHAVIOURS YOU WANT TO CHANGE LATER.

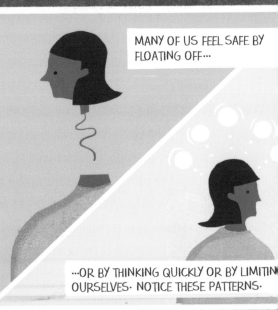

MANY OF US FEEL SAFE BY FLOATING OFF…

…OR BY THINKING QUICKLY OR BY LIMITIN[G] OURSELVES. NOTICE THESE PATTERNS.

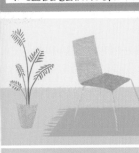

FEEL YOUR FEET

YOU ARE FINE, YOU CAN DO IT

WORK TO CREATE A SAFE SPACE; FIND SAFE PEOPLE, SAY SAFE THINGS. CHANGING THE CONTEXT CAN LEAD TO FEELINGS OF EASE AND COMFORT INSIDE THE BODY.

WHEN YOU CAN CONSISTENT[LY] FIND AT LEAST 3 SIMPLE, RELIABLE, SAFE SENSATIONS INSIDE YOU, YOU ARE GETTIN[G] THE GROUNDING THING.

PERSIST. GROUNDING HELPS YOU FEEL REAL.

'To manage the pain of early trauma, some individuals disconnect from their bodies and live in their minds. They value thinking and logic over feelings and emotions. Other individuals, having never embodied, manage their disconnection by spiritualising their experience...

These individuals tend to live in the energetic field, in more ethereal realms.' P[eople] who are not connected to their bodies 'when asked what are they feeling in their [body] find the question challenging, anxiety provoking, and often impossible to an[swer]' (Heller & LaPierre 2012).

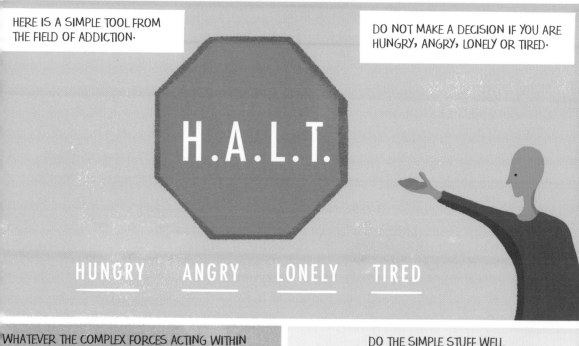

HERE IS A SIMPLE TOOL FROM THE FIELD OF ADDICTION.

DO NOT MAKE A DECISION IF YOU ARE HUNGRY, ANGRY, LONELY OR TIRED.

H.A.L.T.

HUNGRY   ANGRY   LONELY   TIRED

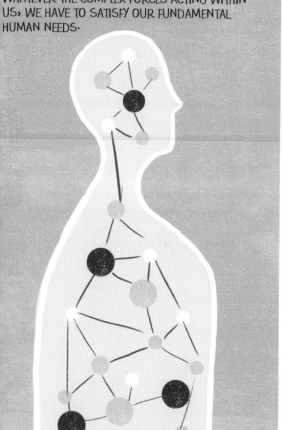

WHATEVER THE COMPLEX FORCES ACTING WITHIN US, WE HAVE TO SATISFY OUR FUNDAMENTAL HUMAN NEEDS.

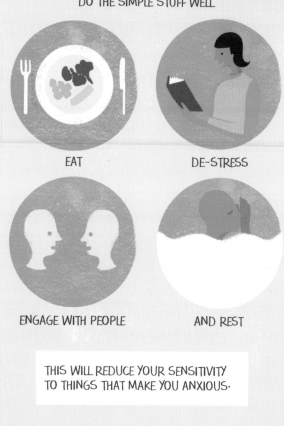

DO THE SIMPLE STUFF WELL

EAT

DE-STRESS

ENGAGE WITH PEOPLE

AND REST

THIS WILL REDUCE YOUR SENSITIVITY TO THINGS THAT MAKE YOU ANXIOUS.

g the right thing" is always context dependent.' 'We are always being shaped
emingly irrelevant stimuli, subliminal information, and internal forces we don't
a thing about' (Sapolsky 2017). For HALT in addiction see Powers (2016).

A 'startling' study showed that judges, paragons of rationality, are meaner if they are hungry or tired. In 2011 researchers reviewed 1100 judicial rulings and found judges were far more likely to grant prisoners parole just after they had eaten or at the start of the day (Sapolsky 2017).

STEPPING OUTSIDE OUR OWN, SEEMINGLY OUT OF CONTROL, PROCESS CAN BE HELPFUL WHEN WE ARE ANXIOUS.

ANY COGNITIVE DISTRACTION, FOR EXAMPLE MAKING LISTS, CAN BE USEFUL, BUT BEING IN NATURE IS THE BEST.

CULTIVATING AWE SLOWS DOWN THE NERVOUS SYSTEM.

CONNECTION TO BODY, CONNECTION TO SELF, CONNECTION TO OTHERS, CONNECTION TO NATURE, CONNECTION TO MYSTERY. THESE ARE ALL INTERWOVEN AND INTERDEPENDENT.

WHEN WAS THE LAST TIME YOU LOOKED AT THE SUNSET OR CHECKED OUT THE STARS OR SIMPLY APPRECIATED YOUR ALIVENESS?

Awe is 'being in the presence of something vast, beyond current understanding'. William James recommended awe to create a ''blissful equanimity'' free from anxieties' (Bergland 2017). Distraction can help anxiety: 'When your thinking brain – the prefrontal cortex – is highly engaged, it slams the brakes on feelings' (Barker 2017).

'Most positive emotions are arousing and engage the "fight-or-flight" response'; 'no awe has the opposite effect'. Awe optimises the control of the heart by increasin activity in the vagus nerve. Research links awe to play, curiosity, imagination, creativity; activities we can all do, even if not outside (Bergland 2017).

REFRAMING IS A TRIED-AND-TESTED TECHNIQUE FOR CHANGING ANXIETY, USED BY PSYCHOLOGISTS AND MINDFULNESS PRACTITIONERS.

IT FITS BEAUTIFULLY WITH THE CONSTRUCTED EMOTION MODEL.

NOTE THE NUANCES AND DETAILS OF THE SENSATIONS INSIDE YOU. TRY 'WHERE DO I FEEL THAT IN MY BODY RIGHT NOW?' NOT 'WHY DO I FEEL ANXIOUS?'

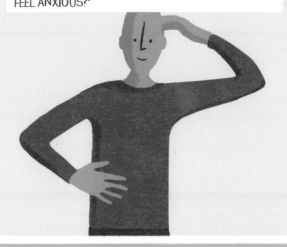

KEEP NOTICING. GO SLOW. CULTIVATE THE GAP BETWEEN PHYSIOLOGICAL SHIFTS AND CO-EMERGING EMOTIONS, THOUGHTS AND MEMORIES.

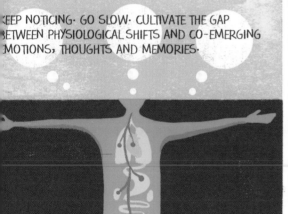

IN THE GAP, CAN YOU REFRAME FEAR TO EXCITEMENT? INSTEAD OF SAYING…

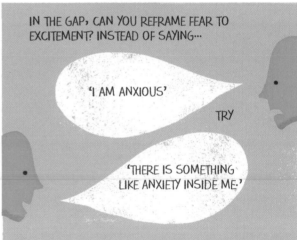

ACKNOWLEDGE THE SIMPLE LOGIC OF YOUR OLD BRAIN. ASK 'WHAT'S THE WORST THING I THINK COULD HAPPEN?'

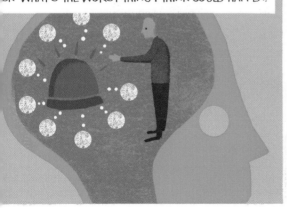

IF YOU ARE FULL OF CATASTROPHIC THOUGHTS, EXPLORE THEM, BUT DO NOT TRUST THEM. KNOW YOUR PRIMITIVE BRAIN IS MISTAKENLY PREDICTING LIFE-OR-DEATH SCENARIOS. GROUND YOURSELF AND CHANGE THE CONTEXT.

because you feel it doesn't make it real. Feelings aren't a satellite dish receiving signals of eternal truth.' 'Change the story and your feelings change' (Barker 2017). If collapse, 'the most potent strategy is to move towards the fear, to contact the immobility itself and to consciously explore the various sensations' (Levine 2010).

'When the body becomes more physiologically regulated', this 'promotes opportunities to feel safe and to develop trusting relationships.' 'Our thoughts can be bolder, more expansive and creative and perhaps even spiritual. These emergent features are not going to be expressed, if we're in the state of constant threat' (Porges 2016).

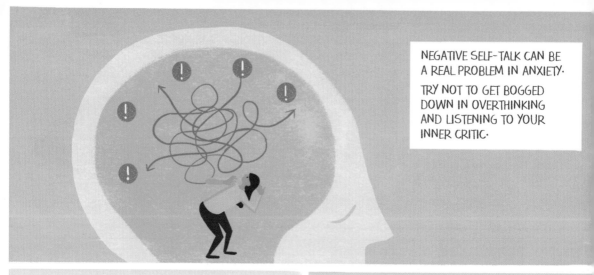

NEGATIVE SELF-TALK CAN BE A REAL PROBLEM IN ANXIETY.

TRY NOT TO GET BOGGED DOWN IN OVERTHINKING AND LISTENING TO YOUR INNER CRITIC.

ANXIETY IS AN OVER-PROTECTIVE FEELING. HAVE SELF-COMPASSION TOWARDS THE CAUTIOUS, FEARFUL PARTS OF YOU, BUT DO NOT FEED THE FLAMES.

CULTIVATE YOUR INNER CHEERLEADER. 'YOU ARE FINE, YOU CAN DO IT.'

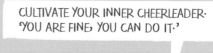

YOU CAN DO IT!

ACT AND MOVE TO BREAK THE CYCLE OF EXCESSIVE RUMINATION.

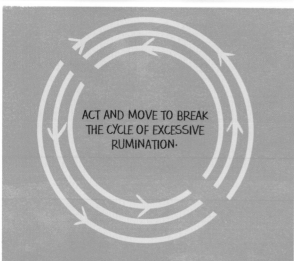

SARTRE URGES ACTION TO ENGAGE IN LIFE: 'I CREATE MYSELF THROUGH WHAT I DO.'

Research shows saying 'you' in self-talk is better than 'I' – weird but true: 'Altogether, the current research showed that second-person self-talk strengthens both actual behavior performance and prospective behavioral intentions more than first-person self-talk' (Dolcos & Albarracin 2014).

Anne Hathaway, filming *Les Misérables*: 'I closed my eyes and I remember think "Hathaway, if you do not do this in this moment, you have no right to call yourself actor. ...just do your job." I opened my eyes and I'm like (snaps fingers): "Let's And I did it' (Dolcos & Albarracin 2014).

TO OVERCOME ANXIETY YOU DO NOT NEED TO REMEMBER OR UNDERSTAND THE CAUSE.

THE GOAL IS TO SELF-REGULATE IN THE PRESENT MOMENT.

HERE ARE SOME REALLY SIMPLE, BODY-BASED TOOLS FOR MANAGING INTENSE SENSATIONS.

ORIENT: SLOWLY TURN YOUR HEAD TO TAKE IN THE SPACE AROUND YOU. NOTICE SOMETHING YOU LIKE IN YOUR IMMEDIATE VICINITY. TRY AGAIN, MORE SLOWLY. WE STIMULATE LOTS OF GREAT REFLEXES THAT PROMOTE FEELING SAFE WHEN WE ORIENT IN THIS WAY.

MOVE: PUSH YOUR FEET INTO THE FLOOR OR, EVEN BETTER, GO INTO A SIMPLE SQUAT POSITION.

TIRE OUT YOUR BIG LEG MUSCLES. REALLY FEEL THE STRENGTH AND POWER IN YOUR LEGS. TRY A FEW TIMES UNTIL YOU UNEQUIVOCALLY FEEL CONNECTED TO YOUR LEGS.

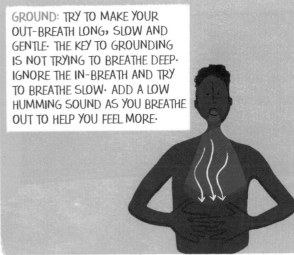

GROUND: TRY TO MAKE YOUR OUT-BREATH LONG, SLOW AND GENTLE. THE KEY TO GROUNDING IS NOT TRYING TO BREATHE DEEP. IGNORE THE IN-BREATH AND TRY TO BREATHE SLOW. ADD A LOW HUMMING SOUND AS YOU BREATHE OUT TO HELP YOU FEEL MORE.

...e storage and flow of information inside us changes as we respond to the world. ...gments of memory that the brain suspects are dangerous can activate anxiety. The ...nger feels real but it's not happening right now. Health is the ability to manage ...ense sensations in the present moment without being overwhelmed.

'Your in-breath will naturally lengthen when your out-breath is longer' (Boyes 2016 and Herrero et al 2017). Levine (2010) recommends the sound 'Voo'; Alexander Technique (Soar 1999) uses 'The Whispered Ah'. Not 'Oh My God' but 'Orient Move Ground'. OMG is explored more fully in *Trauma is Really Strange*.

CHANGING FEELINGS IS OFTEN COUNTER-INTUITIVE. FOR MANY PEOPLE, STRATEGIES ARE BASED ON TRYING TO RELAX OR IGNORE DIFFICULT FEELINGS AS THEY EMERGE.

HERE IS ANOTHER WAY. THINK OF GETTING INTO A CAR AND PUTTING ON YOUR SEAT BELT.

PULLING OPEN THE SEAT BELT IS THE DIRECTION WE WANT TO GO. SIMILAR TO WANTING TO RELAX.

HOWEVER, IF WE PULL TOO HARD AND TOO QUICKLY, THE SEAT BELT LOCKS UP.

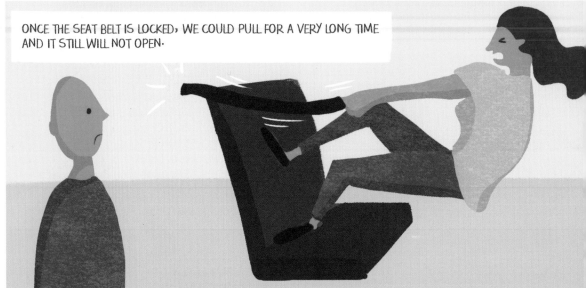

ONCE THE SEAT BELT IS LOCKED, WE COULD PULL FOR A VERY LONG TIME AND IT STILL WILL NOT OPEN.

'Traumatized people chronically feel unsafe inside their bodies: The past is alive in the form of gnawing interior discomfort. Their bodies are constantly bombarded by visceral warning signs, and, in an attempt to control these processes, they often become expert at ignoring their gut feelings and in numbing awareness' (van der Kolk 2015).

An early counter-intuitive approach is 'paradoxical intention' from Viktor Frankl (1 'The phobic patient is invited to intend, even if only for a moment, precisely that w he fears.' By this deliberate engagement 'the wind is taken out of the sails of an See also Wolitzky & Telch (2009) on 'oppositional actions' in exposure.

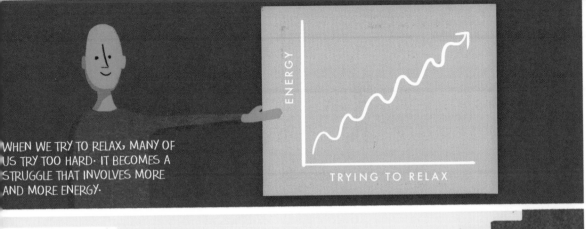

WHEN WE TRY TO RELAX, MANY OF US TRY TOO HARD. IT BECOMES A STRUGGLE THAT INVOLVES MORE AND MORE ENERGY.

A LOCKED SEAT BELT WILL SPRING OPEN, BUT ONLY IF YOU ALLOW IT TO CLOSE FOR A BIT.

SOMETIMES WE NEED TO GO BACKWARDS TO GO FORWARDS. TRY GOING INTO THE DIFFICULT FEELING.

GO SLOW, ALLOW FEELINGS ASSOCIATED WITH DISCHARGING TENSION; IT IS OK TO SHAKE A LITTLE BIT AND BREATHE DIFFERENTLY.

SELF-REGULATE BY PUTTING THE BRAKES ON ANYTHING TOO SPEEDY INSIDE YOU, OR HINTS OF BECOMING DREAMY.

BUT, DO NOT ALWAYS TRY TO RELAX, DO NOT GET STUCK PULLING ON A LOCKED SEAT BELT.

ce we can self-regulate the defence cascade, 'graded exposure' helps in working h anxiety. Pain and anxiety go hand in hand (Granot & Ferber 2005). Think of lding resilience to anxiety as the same as exercising for strength. Graded exposure used to regulate pain and catastrophising (Moseley & Butler 2017).

'Exposure is considered the first-line intervention for anxiety disorders by international health care bodies.' 'The aim of exposure therapy from an inhibitory learning perspective is to help patients generate and strengthen inhibitory associations relative to older fearful associations' (Blakey & Abramowitz 2016).

MOST PEOPLE ASSUME FEELING IS EASY AND NATURAL: IT'S NOT. TO MOVE TOWARDS DIFFICULT FEELINGS AND THEN MOVE AWAY IS A HUGE SKILL.

FEEL A LITTLE BIT OF TENSION AND ANGST IN SHORT BURSTS. PRACTISE IN A CONTEXT WHERE YOU FEEL SAFE, MAYBE WITH A FRIEND.

IF NECESSARY, A BODY-ORIENTED THERAPIST CAN HELP YOU TO FEEL A LITTLE BIT, BUT NOT TOO MUCH.

1 2 3

WHEN STARTING OUT, TRY 30 SECONDS TO 2 MINUTES MAXIMUM FEELING THE DIFFICULT THING. GO REALLY SLOWLY. IN ANY ONE SESSION, EXPLORE FOR 3 SHORT TRIES ONLY, AND THEN REST AND TRY AGAIN ANOTHER DAY.

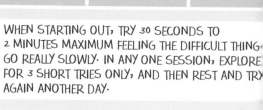

CHALLENGE AND RECOVER, CHALLENGE AND RECOVER. TAKE THE REST PHASES SERIOUSLY.

GOING INTO DIFFICULT FEELINGS CAN BE DONE AS A FORM OF GRADED EXPOSURE.

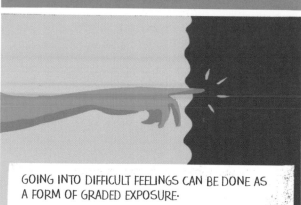

SOMETIMES YOU MAY FEEL WORSE; MAYBE DO LESS NEXT TIME...

...BUT BE PERSISTENT TO DEVELOP RESILIENCE.

THINK OF LEARNING NOT TO PANIC AS LIKE LEARNING TO MAKE LONG TREKS. YOU WILL NEED TO SLEEP WELL, EAT WELL AND PRACTISE. USE A GUIDE WHERE NEEDED AND TRY DIFFERENT ROUTES.

YOU START SLOWLY IN THE 'RECOVERY SPA' AND TAKE YOUR TIME IN THE 'SLOPES OF JUST FEELING SOMETHING'. MAKE SURE YOU AVOID FREEZING 'LAKE DISSOCIATION'.

YOU CAN PROGRESS TO THE 'FOOTHILLS OF SLIGHTLY SCARY AND QUICK'. PRETTY SOON YOU CAN MANAGE 'MOUNT REALLY QUITE ANXIOUS', VISITING THE 'VALLEY OF NAMELESS DREAD' ONLY IF YOU WANT TO.

KEEP GOING AND IT WILL EVEN BE POSSIBLE TO SCALE 'PANIC PEAK' WITHOUT FEAR.

THEY ARE ALL FEELINGS, CONSTRUCTED INSIDE YOU.

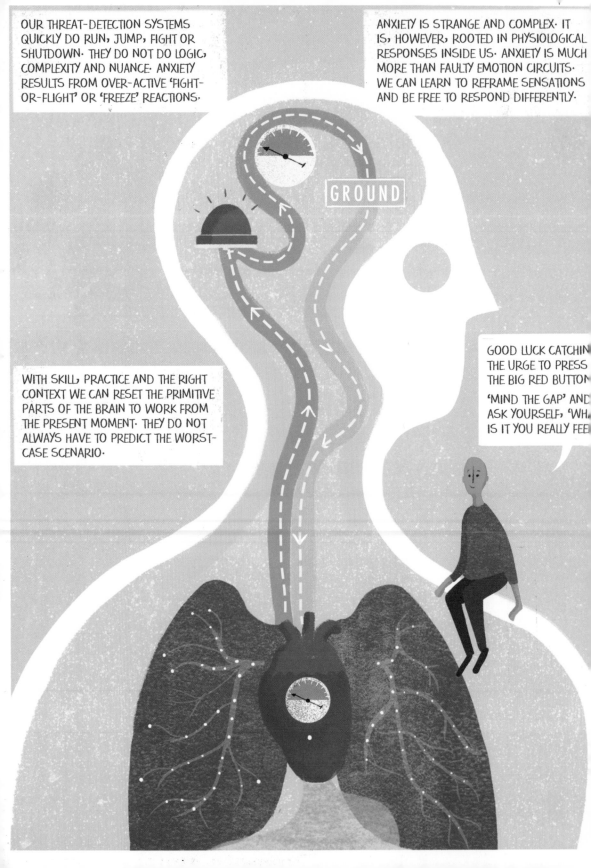